Scriptures taken from the Holy Bible, New International Reader's Version®, NIrV® Copyright © 1995, 1996, 1998 by Biblica, Inc.™ Used by permission of Zondervan.**www.zondervan.com** The "NIrV" and "New International Reader's Version" are trademarks registered in the United States Patent and Trademark Office by Biblica, Inc.™
Scriptures taken from the Holy Bible, New International Version®, NIV®. Copyright © 1973, 1978, 1984, 2011 by Biblica, Inc.™ Used by permission of Zondervan. All rights reserved worldwide. **www.zondervan.com** The "NIV" and "New International Version" are trademarks registered in the United States Patent and Trademark Office by Biblica, Inc.™
Scripture taken from The Expanded Bible. Copyright ©2011 by Thomas Nelson. Used by permission. All rights reserved.
Scripture quotations are from the ESV® Bible (The Holy Bible, English Standard Version®), copyright © 2001 by Crossway, a publishing ministry of Good News Publishers. Used by permission. All rights reserved."
Scripture quotations from THE MESSAGE. Copyright © by Eugene H. Peterson 1993, 1994, 1995, 1996, 2000, 2001, 2002. Used by permission of NavPress. All rights reserved. Represented by Tyndale House Publishers, Inc.

Cover design: Jenni Hoekstra
Interior Design: Mark Rueben
Editor: Various, with special thanks to the #4500

Swearingen-Friesen, Nadia, 1967-
Devotional Readings for Decisions That Make a Difference
ISBN 978-0-9963538-2-3

All websites and contact information listed herein are accurate at the time of publication, but may change in the future or cease to exist. The listing of website references are for informational purposes and listing does not imply endorsement of their activities.

We hope that you enjoy this book from Four Hope Publishers. Our goal is to provide thought-provoking and encouraging books and products that will empower parents to approach the raising of their children in an intentional and nurturing manner.

Four Hope
Publishing

Chicago, IL

Printed in the United States of America

Devotional Readings
For

Decisions
That Make
A
Difference

Introduction

This devotional reading was written to supplement one of my popular speaking topics, *Decisions that Make a Difference*, soon to be a book all its own. You don't need to have heard the talk or read the book to benefit from the devotions. But it is an important thing to think through.

We make hundreds of decisions daily. As parents, we are faced with choices to make, details to tend to, and arguments to settle, every single day. From what to feed our family to appropriate clothing for teens, we are slogging through a minefield of rights and wrongs and yeses and nos while struggling to keep our focus on the things that matter in the face of so much distraction.

It often feels like a job we will never master. And maybe we won't.

But, this I know for sure, there are decisions that *make a difference*. There are areas that need our focus that will literally impact the path our children will someday choose. There are lessons we must teach and discipline we must offer and attention that is sorely needed to bring our kids from infancy to adulthood. The job is huge. But not overwhelming.

Because the truth of the matter is that it is not an accident that you have been entrusted with your child. You are, even on the hardest day, the exact right person to raise your baby up, not to be a good kid, but to be a faithful, capable, loving adult. You are that parent.

Maybe you need to regroup. Maybe you feel like the day-to-day schedule of living with littles has taken from you all that you hoped you could be.

Or maybe you find yourself at a place where the world of parenting has just been too hard. You can no longer discern what matters and what is just another choice on another ordinary day.

Perhaps you feel you are doing okay but you want to remember what actually matters so that you can keep on *keeping on.*

You are standing in exactly the right spot.

Even if you do not believe that truth.

It is time for us to set aside the wild distraction that bombards us every single day. It is time for us to rise up and remember that even on the longest day, our years with these children are short. It is time for us to focus anew on knowing what we believe and finding deeper strength to grasp on to these things so that we can help our children grow into the adults they are meant to be.

It is time.

And this is a beginning.

Each devotional reading below will include a Bible verse and some thoughts for you to reflect upon. There is a prayer at the end and a place for you to write some prayer requests of your own. Be specific and think about what that reading has nudged in you. You will also find a section following each reading that offers a couple ideas you may want to try.

As you go through these readings, please offer yourself grace. Every parent, everywhere, is working on their own struggles. No one has arrived. You are in very good company, no matter where you are. Fight the urge to become overwhelmed.

If there is anything I have learned as I parent my four, it is that no good growth or joyful work comes from the weight of being overwhelmed. Consider one small thing you might like to try or adjust in your own life. Start with a small thing and work on from there. Becoming the parent you want to be does not happen overnight. Not for any of us. And the truth is that most will never fully achieve that goal. But can we do a little better today than yesterday? This is possible!

Think it through a bit at a time. There are decisions we make that truly matter, that truly make a difference in the life of our family.

Let's begin to think about those.

First Things First

PSALM 86:11

NEW INTERNATIONAL READER'S VERSION
(NIRV)

LORD, TEACH ME HOW YOU WANT ME TO LIVE.
DO THIS SO THAT I WILL DEPEND ON YOU,
MY FAITHFUL GOD.
GIVE ME A HEART THAT DOESN'T WANT
ANYTHING
MORE THAN TO WORSHIP YOU.

There is no way we can teach our children how to live until we have thought about this ourselves. There is no way we can tell them what matters in life, if the lives we live tell a different story. We have to find a way to understand what God wants *us* to do, how he wants us to live, what he wants us to value, before we can help our children do the same.

And so what is that thing?

Ask yourself, what am I called to do? Am I moving toward that purpose? What am I called to value? Does my bank account tell that tale? Does my daily calendar?

Years ago, after living in ministry for a long while,

my husband and I felt called to leave that work. It was a gut-wrenching decision for us though we knew it was the right choice. As we said our good-byes and prepared for a completely different lifestyle, I found myself struggling to understand what God wanted me to do next. Why would he call us away from a life-style of outreach and compassion? I would soon find myself at home with two preschoolers and no ministry at hand.

I felt lost.

As I struggled with the impending move, I came face to face with the fact that I truly did not see raising my children as a ministry opportunity. Somehow I had come to a place where I understood outreach as something we did with and for others. It had nothing at all to do with our immediate family.

And I was wrong.

Through spiritual wrestling and earnest prayer, I could feel God correcting my view. Raising my children in faith would be my big work now and for a season to come. And that was valuable and needed and could potentially impact a world far bigger than my family. Intentionally raising my children to see the world through a faithful lens could lead them to take their place in the work God will bring them to when they are grown. Even more importantly, I could help my children understand that they have a role to play in that Kingdom. Not only in the far future, but right away, today.

This was at the core of what God was teaching me during that time of transition.

I have a role to play.

And I want to do it well.

In order to raise our children to understand the world around them, in order to bring them into an understanding of the part that faith plays in the life we will live, we need to look and think and wrestle and rest in God's truth.

The wonder of this whole thing is that we do not need to have all the answers. We need only teach the questions. What do we ask? Where do we see God's hand? What would he have us do? Asking these, and teaching our children to do the same, makes it possible for our kids to grow up seeking to look at their lives through the lens of faith.

Life was meant to be lived with the truth of our faith woven into every area. Our beliefs, when left to live on Sundays alone, are weakened, restricted. As parents, we must allow the truth of God's grace and his deep love for us to flow from Sunday into Monday and on throughout the week. We must model for our children the way that faith offers a light into darkened times, the way our beliefs inform our decision-making, the way God himself can be welcomed in the ordinary moments of our regular lives.

When they see this, they will follow.

And isn't that just what we would like?

Prayer: Dear God, help me see your hand in my own life so that I can help my children see you moving in theirs. I want my faith to be a part of every day and I want to rely on you for strength and wisdom as I seek to raise my children well. Thank you for your grace to me. In Jesus' name, Amen.

Prayer Request:

Two Things to Try:

1. Have a favorite verse? Post it in your house in a place you see often. Looking for a verse? I like Psalm 16.

2. Affirm your child by noticing a God-given gift that is a part of their personality. Help them to see that God has created them to be exactly who they are.

Faith Matters

Proverbs 22:6

English Standard Version (ESV)

Train up a child in the way he should
go;
even when he is old he will not
depart from it.

Maybe you grew up in a home of faith. Maybe you did not. Regardless of what you were taught or what you believe, one thing is true: You were created to be a spiritual being. Your mind and body, your very self, was made with a need to connect to God. This is true for you and it is surely true for your children, as well.

Growing up, we did not attend church. I did not know who or what God was. And yet, I can clearly remember sitting in my room when my parents were in a heated argument, and wondering if God could help. On my bed, in a light blue room, I prayed without knowing what prayer was. Without any formal teaching about faith, the need and desire to know God was already present. We are made that way, you and I.

But what do we do with this knowledge? How do we proceed from here?

As parents, we have been entrusted with an enormous task. These children we adore need to be nurtured and loved and trained and taught. They need to grow into a deep understanding of both who they are and *whose* they are. Achieving this work will take us far more days than we have been given. So, this I know for sure: We do not have time to waste.

We must dig deep and rise up and find small, intentional ways to pour into our children daily. When we are tired and when we are weary, we must choose to stand firm and tend to the task at hand anyway. And somehow, as we process through the trying days of parenting, we have to set aside the distractions that abound and focus on those things that truly matter. We must find ways to make *decisions that make a difference.*

Raising a child in faith is definitely one of these.

So on this very day, we must set our minds and choose. On this very day, we will abolish the thought that doing anything ourselves is *easier*. And we will remember that we did not become parents to do the easy thing. When we look into the faces of our kids today, we will speak truth to them and over them and around them and about them. We will allow our faith to be lived out in ways that they can see and feel; in ways that show our belief in the Creator God, in his saving Son, in the sustaining Spirit.

And we will do this today because *this day matters.*

Whether your child is three months, years or decades old, your teaching is bringing him into a deeper understanding of who God is. Your words and compassion and example of grace will take root in her young life and from there, it can grow into a belief system that offers peace, guidance and salvation that will last far longer than you.

Isn't this just what we want?

The verse above is taken from the English Standard Version of The Bible. Another translation, The Message, puts it this way:

Point your kids in the right direction—
when they're old they won't be lost.

So, whether we are walking outside or tending to tasks at home, today let's point out where we see God in the world around us. Whether this is found in the wonder of nature or the miracle of ten tiny toes, let's help our children see that truth. Today, let's allow our children to see us prioritize prayer and read Scripture. Let's figure out where we can foster our faith in word and action so that they see the way we have chosen. Today and tomorrow and from now on, let's point them in the right direction.

No matter how old your child is, you can impact them by paying attention to this decision that makes a difference. Share your faith. Teach them truth. Help them to know that they were created to be in relationship with God.

Just like you.

Just like me.

Prayer: Dear Heavenly Father, give me wisdom today as I seek to bring my child closer to you. Draw us near. Fill in the rough places where I try and sometimes fail. And help me to see and accept that we were all made to be in relationship with you. I need you, Lord. Thank you for your grace and for your love. In Jesus' name, Amen.

Prayer Requests:

Two Things to Try:

1. Pray with your child at a time other than bed or meal time. Help them to see that we can talk to God at all times of day.

2. Share with your family one place where you saw God working today.

Prioritize Teaching

DEUTERONOMY 11:18-21

NEW INTERNATIONAL VERSION (NIV)

18 Fix these words of mine in your hearts and minds; tie them as symbols on your hands and bind them on your foreheads. 19 Teach them to your children, talking about them when you sit at home and when you walk along the road, when you lie down and when you get up. 20 Write them on the doorframes of your houses and on your gates, 21 so that your days and the days of your children may be many in the land the Lord swore to give your ancestors, as many as the days that the heavens are above the earth.

As we seek to be parents who understand the importance of our work, we need to ask ourselves not just what needs to be done but how do we do it? How do we focus on the things that matter and raise our children up to be both educated and wise?

It is absolutely imperative that we help our families to see and understand the world from a view of faith. Our kids will take the faith we share with them into their lives outside our home. They will use that faith to engage with others socially, to understand their academic education and to find their way in the world. As they grow and develop their belief system, they will learn to see where God is in the whole of it.

And He is there. Always. There is nothing at all that is outside of the reach of His hand. But how do we take our belief systems and empower our kids to use them outside of church?

We seek to raise children of faith. To do this, we must understand the importance of fostering curiosity. We want to help our kids seek knowledge and wisdom. We want to listen and see what areas of life light up their eyes. As they learn at home and at school, they come closer and closer to understanding the direction God would like them to take someday. And as all of this unfolds, we must teach them to see what they are learning through the lens of faith.

When my firstborn, Noah, began middle school, he believed he was bad at math. When I shared this with his teacher, a goal was set to make math a strength. As Noah grew in confidence, he found himself exposed to new opportunities and began to consider future careers that had never been possibilities before. When an engineer came to present during a Career Day event, Noah was amazed. God opened his eyes and he suddenly knew what he wanted to do. From that day forward, his educational decisions were made with an eye upon graduating from college with an engineering degree. As I write this, Noah is completing his freshman year in college as a Mechanical Engineering student at a Christian university. And while it may not seem to you that this has anything to do with Noah's belief in God, we know that nothing is outside of God's dominion. Our son can use his passion for math and science to pursue engineering and in doing so, contribute to God's Kingdom here on earth.

I truly believe that in the midst of that Career Day event, Noah's academic education intersected with his faith journey. Both his faith and his education came together in a way that allowed him to see a glimpse of what his future might entail. As his parents, if we had we left either of these aspects under-developed, he may have missed that light-bulb moment altogether.

It is so important that we not delegate the task of teaching our children to someone else. We must remain involved and process what they are experiencing at school. We need to foster good habits in school-and in faith-and be ready to help our children find their way in the world. While all this is happening, our kids will hear the beliefs and views of teachers, friends, pastors, and family members. All of these opinions can muddy the waters *or* create clarity but it is absolutely essential that we foster an ongoing conversation to help our children learn to see and understand their world.

And so we talk to them at home and make our faith known. We draw them to the Bible in story and in grace. We pray with and for them, *especially for them*. The God of all, who knows this day and all of the ones to come, will meet us where we are as we seek to train our children in faith. Our attention to education and faith will teach them deep understanding of what it means to own a Christian world-and-life-view. In understanding the world around them, our children will begin to understand their place in it all.

So today, go outside and marvel at creation. Wonder at the size of the universe and the creativity of God who, with his own hands, created both Pluto and platypus. Connect to compassion and allow your children to follow the lead of the Spirit as they experience the desire to help those in need.

Teach them *intentionally* to value education, to

seek it diligently and to learn to see what they are learning as a part of their faithful journey.

Prayer: Dear Jesus, we love you. We want to raise our family in such a way that they can act upon that love daily. We want them to grow in wisdom and faith and we want them to seek knowledge so that they can find their way to what it is that you have for them to do here on earth. Help us to be diligent and to teach diligence. In Your name alone, Amen.

Prayer Requests:

Two Things to Try:

1. Refrain from asking your children what they learned at school today. Instead, ask them to tell you something they found interesting, something they read or something that was confusing to them at school.

2. Consider reading a book with your child,

regardless of their age. Share the story together and then plan a follow up activity that correlates to the book.

Love with Abandon

PSALM 103:17

EXPANDED BIBLE (EXB)

*17 BUT THE LORD'S LOVE FOR THOSE WHO
RESPECT HIM
CONTINUES FOREVER AND EVER,
AND HIS GOODNESS CONTINUES TO THEIR
GRANDCHILDREN.*

When Mark and I began our family, we were given a beautiful, white Scottish lace blanket as a gift at a baby shower. It was the softest thing I have ever felt. When Noah was born, it became the one thing he could not be without. He slept with it, learned to walk with it, cried into it. Over time, the white gave way to gray and holes formed and no matter how it looked or what shape it took, he loved it all the more. He never sought the perfection that it had once held. He never noticed that its softness had been rubbed off. All he saw was his most beloved treasure. That blanket became a part of his story and something he always held near.

That blanket reminds me of a deep, important truth. I want to remind myself and I want to remind you because understanding this sits at the core of who we are.

Understanding this makes it possible for us to love others with abandon.

The truth is you are loved. Deeply LOVED. If you were lost, you would be sought and brought back near. And it does not matter that you have not *arrived.* You are certainly not who you were. You are loved in this moment, exactly as you are.

Yes, *this* is truth.

And it is from this truth that we come to understand ourselves, as God understands us. If we are so deeply loved, then we must have worth. Maybe your life circumstances make this hard to imagine or maybe you have been told differently, but nothing can change the way God loves his children. It is not because of what you do that he adores you so. Instead, it is because you are his.

Perhaps your child has a lovey like the blanket that Noah loved. Once upon a time, that lovey was shiny and new. Once upon a time, it held clean colors and exact shapes. Now, if *you* look at it through your eyes, you may see the tattered edges and used up bits. If you look with human sight, you see the object from outside. It does not belong to you.

For your child, however, it is a very different

story.

Your child loves that item because it is his. Your child sees with perfect sight that loving this one thing has made it what it is today. It is warm and familiar and comforting and good. It is irreplaceable and entirely hers. It is valued, not due to external perfection, but because of the worth it has in the eyes of your child.

In the eyes of God, you are valuable. You are loved. You are worth far more than you can understand. He knows every detail of you and does not love in spite of these idiosyncrasies, but *because of them*. And when we understand this, we are able to shower our children with love because we understand deeply what it means. The overwhelming adoration that God offers creates an overflow of love that can wash over us and on to those we adore. Understanding how we are seen by God literally gives us access to the love we want to shower on our children.

And this, our children need.

Every day, they need to be touched, to be adored, to be seen, to be valued. It is in receiving all of this from those they trust that they can grow into a deeper understanding of themselves. As they mature and learn about their own worth, they can then connect with others and offer their gifts and skills to a greater community. They open themselves to the love you offer and begin to learn, by your example, what it means to be loved by God.

It is big, important work, this.

So, make a decision to begin today. Pull your baby close. With their head in your hands, speak words of affirmation and adoration over the one you love. Tousle the hair of your teen, pull your child in for a hug, tell them again and again and again that they are loved right where they are.

This is a sacred task.

Prayer: Dear Jesus, thank you for your love. Thank you for seeing me, with all my imperfections, and loving me still. Help me to shower affection on my family and give me all that they need to grow into the people you need them to become. Give me wisdom as I seek to create a home that will offer security and hope. In your name alone, Amen.

Prayer Requests:

Two Things to Try:

1. Make a point of maintaining eye contact with your child today. Encourage them to look at your face, too.

2. Intentionally reach out and touch your child. Tousling hair or offering a hug can help you feel connected to your child and can help them feel loved. (Even teens need this.)

Teach Discernment

EPHESIANS 6:4

THE MESSAGE (MSG)

*4 FATHERS, DON'T EXASPERATE YOUR
CHILDREN BY COMING DOWN HARD
ON THEM.*

*TAKE THEM BY THE HAND AND LEAD
THEM IN THE WAY OF THE MASTER.*

A wide variety of media brings images and sounds of what the world can be. It shows us how to dress, ways to respond, attitudes to emulate, lifestyles to pursue. Every sound byte and perfected picture is presented to us from a specific worldview. And all of it draws us closer, or farther, from the God who loves us so.

This is true for our children, as well.

We have been given a great task. Our children, entrusted to us, are in need of teaching, guidance, wisdom. And in the absence of these, they will find direction for their lives in the media that bombards them daily.

Whether your child is 2 or 12 or 22, they are

processing the world around them and trying to find their place. They are looking for messages to help them understand what they believe and what truth is. And there is no voice that will hold greater meaning to them than yours. None. Even when they roll their eyes and turn their heads, even when they choose differently, it is your voice and your teaching that will echo deep inside.

So, we must teach.

We must teach them the difference between right and wrong and give them the whys behind this teaching. We must help them place their feet upon the path of righteousness and keep on putting them back in that place when their choices send them left or right.

We must help them comprehend the images and sounds that media offers from a deep understanding of faith. We do all this so they can see the world around them through the lens of scripture.

But this great work cannot be done in raised voices and random commands. This work must be approached with great tenderness and divine direction. Our children need us to come alongside them and offer understanding. Our children need us to base our teaching in relationship and love instead of punishment and control.

They need to know that we understand the draw to be *part* of the world, while they learn that there is another way. They need to know that we are educated and knowledgeable about what is current in culture and then learn how to apply their faith to their choices.

This is not an easy thing to do.

When we are weary, the job continues. When we are failing, the job continues. When we lose our own way and find ourselves lured toward things that fly in the face of our faith, the job continues. We do not have the luxury of apathy. Our children need to know how to understand the world around them and they need to know how all this intersects with their faith.

So raise the bar high for their behavior and clothing choices and music downloads and friends. Raise the bar high for your own responses, your gentle teaching and the valuing of this work above whatever distractions arise.

It is our voices they keep.

What will you teach them today?

Prayer: Dear Lord, give me wisdom to help my

children understand the world in which we live. Help me to know what things we must remove from our family life and what things we can allow. Give me wisdom as I seek to raise my children up in a way that allows them to understand the world but not succumb to those things which will keep them far from you. Thank you for hearing me and thank you for this task. Help me to do it well. In Jesus' Name, Amen.

Prayer Requests:

Two Things to Try:

1. Ask your child to teach you how to play their favorite video game. Many games are based in story. What story will they tell?

2. Watch a television program together. Process the program with your child. What do they see? What behaviors are present? Do they agree with these? Help them to see the program through "faith goggles" without

preaching to your child. Ask clarifying questions, instead.

Delighting in Distraction

1JOHN 3:7-8

NEW INTERNATIONAL READER'S VERSION
(NIRV)

*7 Dear children, don't let anyone lead
you astray. The person who does what
is right is holy, just as Christ is
holy. 8 The person who does what is
sinful belongs to the devil. That's
because the devil has been sinning
from the beginning. But the Son of God
came to destroy the devil's work.*

Sometimes, when the light of truth burns our eyes,
we recoil from the shock… and then act offended. Truth
can sting and we want to defend ourselves, even when we
know we are wrong.

Recently I polled a large group of parents asking
them what causes them to lose their focus on making solid
decisions that make a difference in the lives of their
families. I anticipated a set of answers that seemed most
likely. What I got was wholly different.

"I log onto Facebook and lose track of time."

"The constant availability my phone provides

steals time from my children."

"Video-gaming takes up way more time than I would like…"

"Technology fills my day and much of what I know I should tend to is left undone."

"I am allowing myself to be distracted by a million little, meaningless things."

Does any of this ring true for you?

This is a difficult subject to think about because it cuts to the core of many adults today. The reality is that we are raising our children at a very different time and in a wildly different culture than the one in which we were raised.

Our parents had struggles and distractions that took their attention, and their own goals for child-rearing. However, with the growth of social media and technology options, we are inundated with information and requests for attention at all times of the day and night. And yet our children need not only our presence but our *attention*. They need to be seen and heard and noticed and raised in very hands-on ways. The little actions of affection that had been commonplace before the onslaught of all things electronic are lost in today's society and our children are paying the price.

My friend, Kris, was brought up by a loving mom who always offered a warm smile whenever she caught Kris' eye. One day, while entertaining guests at home, Kris came into the room and looked up at her mom. In her busyness, her mom nodded, but did not smile. Kris immediately burst into tears. She felt suddenly and overwhelming snubbed, unloved, unseen.

Not all children can tell a story like the one Kris told me. But all children do have similar needs. If we do not stop to look at them, touch them, interact with them intentionally, how will they know to offer anyone the same? What will this do to the relationships they will form as adults? What will it do to the efforts they make as parents?

What we do today matters. We have been given a great responsibility and we must tend to it intentionally. We are being led astray, a little bit at a time, by the delight of distraction and in allowing this to happen, we are releasing ourselves from the responsibility with which we have been entrusted.

Every single day, we are called to make many decisions. Some of these truly matter. Some of these will decide the direction our children choose to pursue. We have the ability to teach our children to know and follow God, to love others and themselves, to find balance in how they use technology or engage in the mundane. We have this one chance to teach them that all of this *matters*. We have this one chance to teach them to find balance before they risk losing their footing and begin to approach decisions with an apathetic attitude.

What will we choose?

If we sat down, you and I, and asked each other these questions face-to-face, I am sure the words we would choose would state our commitment to parenting well. But, do our actions line up with our words? Are we living what we believe is important? Do we model it more often than not?

Because the truth is we will never get it done perfectly. And this is not the goal for which we strive. What we need to earnestly seek after is a desire to do what we can on this one day. It is a raising of the bar, an expecting of better, even while knowing that we will often fall short. What our children need from us is to love them in a way that leads them and prepares them to be more than well-behaved kids.

We are not in the business of raising good kids.

No.

We are working to raise faithful, compassionate, loving adults.

The baby in your arms and the child at your feet and the teen on the couch will not stay as they are today. We are on our way. You and me both. These children will grow up and they will move on and they will take their place in the world.

What do we need to teach them while we have them close?

The sheer delight of distraction is keeping us from those lessons, that goal. And we need to find a better way.

And yes, this may feel offensive. It stings. I feel it, too.

But we do not have the days to waste indignantly stomping our foot over our own self-righteousness. Instead, we need to draw a line in the sand. Where will that line fall for you? What small change do you need to make today? Write it here. Claim it.

Now, we go forward. Sting and all.

Prayer: Dear God, my attention is drawn to a million tiny things all the time. I am tied to technology and have fallen prey to the tyranny of the urgent. Sometimes, I cannot even remember what I am working toward. Help me to hear your voice. Help me to know your dreams for our family. Help me to focus on the most important thing and set my goals to tend to that. Forgive me for allowing myself to be led astray. Thank you for your grace. Help me to shower that grace on others, as well. In Jesus' name, Amen.

Prayer requests:

Two Things to Try:

1. Evaluate your own distractions. What parameters can you put in place to reduce these?

2. Spend time together as a family without the

distractions of phones. Do one activity together for at least 30 minutes. Intentionally be present during that time.

Parent or Friend?

DEUTERONOMY 4:8-10

NEW INTERNATIONAL VERSION (NIV)

9 Only be careful, and watch yourselves closely so that you do not forget the things your eyes have seen or let them fade from your heart as long as you live. Teach them to your children and to their children after them.

My husband often tells a story about a Saturday morning outing to a restaurant when our two small sons misbehaved throughout breakfast and then again on the ride home. At the restaurant, they were given helium balloons in two different colors. As we began our drive home, the boys argued about who would keep which balloon and we could hear a sense of entitlement growing in their preschool minds. We corrected them several times, reminding them that they were lucky to have gotten the balloons at all. The arguing continued. We told them it wasn't too late to let them go but they continued to misbehave. In Mark's words:

They called my bluff.

I stopped the truck.

"Hand me the balloons", I said.

Their eyes grew wide but not yet believing. I opened the door and got out, then opened the back door so they could watch the scene unfold.

Holding one string in my left hand, the other in my right, I turned to my boys and advised them to say goodbye to their balloons. Two mouths dropped open beneath wide, unblinking eyes – eyes still not quite believing but horrified at the possibility.

I lifted both arms high above my head.

And let go.

This story has become something of a legend in our home. If our younger two children begin to argue in entitled tones, our two balloon-less boys (now taller than I by far) will quickly remind them of this tale and encourage them to be grateful for all they have.

All these many years later, they remember still. And they know that their parents will make the hard choice. They know that we are not so impacted by the desire to be liked that we will overlook a teaching opportunity. Even if that opportunity leads to many minutes of tears.

Your children may have many friends. They will make acquaintances in a variety of places. They will hang out with folks who will laugh with them and make memories or who perhaps will fall away. There are and will be people in their lives who come and go and *not even one of them* will ever hold the place you hold. Not one of these others, no matter how special, can ever claim what you yourself can claim. You are your child's *parent.*

The origin of this word is so important. Coming from Latin, *parentem* translates as ancestor. Another root, *Parerer,* means to bring forth, to produce. You are, indeed, the ancestor who produces or brings forth your child, your family. Whether through birth or adoption, you have literally created a family by parenting children. This is a sacred and personal thing that only you can own.

If this is true, then why do we sometimes feel the need to *also* be our child's friend?

As our children are growing up, it is *not our job* to be their bud. Our work is far more important than that. Our job is teach and admonish, to love and discipline, to praise and correct. Our job is to give them our own teaching based in experience and wisdom, our own voice that will play in their heads for a lifetime.

Throughout their lives, our kids will meet people who seek to be liked, who do similar activities, who are at the same developmental stage. They aim to please, to entertain, to impress. None of this relates to our calling as parents.

We have intentionally put ourselves in a position to live life alongside these little people who will disagree with us, disobey us, and are developmentally in a wildly different stage. If our goal is to be liked, we are going to find ourselves in a very difficult place. Instead, we must find our self-worth elsewhere and prepare ourselves to make decisions that are very unpopular with the people we deeply love. We must sort through our own life experiences and, remembering what lessons we have learned, offer them to our children with an eye trained on the big picture. *We are bringing them up.* We are creating a family. We are preparing young children to grow into wise adults.

The work is big. And it is solely yours.

You do not need to be a friend to your children. Their friends will never have the impact on their lives that you have. Their friends will never be as committed to their upbringing as you are. Their position in the lives of your children is utterly different and seeking to take that place, as well as your own, hampers your ability to teach and raise your kids. As you go through life with your littles, you will have to say the hard things, correct and sometimes offend. You will have to fight for better behavior, higher standards, clearer morals than a friend might ever do. You will do it selflessly, pouring into your kids in a way that buddies and acquaintances do not consider.

All of this must happen without fearing the falling out. You cannot parent wisely out of fear. Instead, you have to trust that being a person of integrity who loves her family with abandon will someday allow you to have a relationship with an adult child that is warm and friendly…

But truth be told, it will always be *more than that.*

So, stand up tall and say no to things that are contrary to the goals you have for your kids. Say no to inappropriate video games and immodest clothes. Say no to being cool and no to acting like a kid and no to trying to impress and no to so many other things that will keep you from doing what *you alone* can do.

And then settle yourself in for a ride.

The God of all of creation has his hands all over your family. He sees what you have to offer and what you need to find. He pours his grace freely and lovingly into all the spaces that you cannot fill. And he intends it all for good. Though you may sometimes feel alone, this is never the truth. He is walking alongside you and offering you strength for whatever may be ahead.

Embrace the position you have been given. Your child will never have another person who can stand where you stand. It is hard and beautiful, holy and gritty.

Exactly as it is supposed to be.

Prayer: Dear Jesus, help me to not want to prioritize the "cool parent" over the good one. Develop in me the desire to be wise. Give me the strength to accept the position you have given me in the life of my child and guide me as I seek to use what I know of you to draw them closer to you every day. Thank you for your grace. In Jesus' name, Amen.

Prayer Requests:

Two Things to Try:

1. Think of experiences your family shares
    together that are specific only to you.
    Hardships, celebrations, losses or events that
    matter to you differently than the rest of the
    world. Affirming these shared experiences can
    help us to understand our relationship to one
    another.

2. When you have the need to correct someone in
    your family today, be intentional about doing
    so with a calm voice and an eye toward
    teaching. Your role in the life of your child is
    important. Nurture their growth gentle and
    purposefully today.

Resources

If you are looking for resources related to some of the readings included here, I recommend the following.

The first is a helpful website that offers parents a better understanding of a wide variety of media sources.

The second is my first book which offers hope for families living in survival mode.

Family, Focus on the. *http://www.pluggedin.com/*. n.d.

Swearingen-Friesen, Nadia. *Sticks! A Practical Way to Reduce Stress, Improve Discipline and Create the Family You Want*. Chicago, IL: Four Hope Publishing, 2015.

From the Author

I'd love to hear about how these readings have connected with you personally. We are all working through this, one step at a time. This is true for you and for me, as well.

You can find me online. On my website – www.NadiaSwearingen-Friesen.com – you can drop me a note, locate additional resources, read my latest blog, and check out my speaking topics and upcoming events.

You can also follow me on these social media sites:

Facebook: www.Facebook.com/nadialisesf
Twitter: @NadiaLise
Instagram: NadiaLiseSF
Pinterest: NadiaLise
Periscope: @NadiaLise

Whether I hear from you or not, I wish you blessings and perseverance in your family's journey. Remember, small changes often make a big difference!

Nadia